Dear Mary and H

This remind... me of our wonderful trip in the South of France. " Simplicity is the keynote of Elegance."

Love to you both,

Sarah Jane

WE COULD ALMOST
EAT OUTSIDE

PHILIPPE DELERM

WE COULD ALMOST EAT OUTSIDE

An Appreciation of Life's Small Pleasures

Translated from the French by Sarah Hamp

PICADOR USA

NEW YORK

Book design by Julie Duquet
Illustrations © 1999 by Sally Mara Sturman

Library of Congress Cataloging-in-Publication Data

Delerm, Philippe, 1950–
    [La première gorgée de bière et autres plaisirs minuscules. English]
    We could almost eat outside : an appreciation of life's small pleasures / Philippe Delerm.
        p. cm.
    ISBN 0-312-20364-0
    I. Title.
PQ2664.E5155P7413   1999
844'.914—dc21   99-25536
                                                            CIP

First published in France under the title *La première gorgée de bière et autres plaisirs minuscules* by Editions Gallimard

First published in Great Britain under the title *The Small Pleasures of Life* by Phoenix House

FIRST PICADOR USA EDITION: JUNE 1999

10   9   8   7   6   5   4   3   2   1

Contents

WE COULD ALMOST
EAT OUTSIDE

A Knife in Your Pocket

It CERTAINLY ISN'T A kitchen knife. And it can't be a switchblade. But it's not a penknife either. So let's agree on an Opinel No. 6, or a Laguiole pocketknife. The sort of knife you could picture belonging to a perfect, imaginary grandfather. A knife he'd have slipped into his thick-ribbed, chocolate-brown corduroys. A knife he'd have pulled out of his pocket at lunchtime, impaling slices of *saucisson* on its tip, or wrapping his fingers around its blade as he carefully peeled an apple. The sort of knife which, once he'd drained the coffee from his cup, he'd have made a great show of closing—this being the signal for everyone to return to work.

I'm thinking of the sort of knife you dreamed about as a child: a knife fit to hew a bow and arrow, or to fashion a wooden sword with a bark hilt—the sort your parents always insisted was too dangerous for children.

And the purpose of this knife? For they don't make grandfathers like that anymore, and you're no longer a child. A virtual knife then, with this lame excuse: "But you never know when it might come in handy—walks, picnics, even the odd job around the house when there aren't any other tools around . . ."

Of course you know you'll never use it. The pleasure lies elsewhere. In the selfish enjoyment of its aesthetic, its exotic wood or shiny mother-of-pearl handle, its cabalistic emblem—on the blade, a hand encircled by a crown, an umbrella, a nightingale, on the handle a bee. Symbol of a simpler life, nurturing a deeply satisfying sort of prejudice. In the age of the fax, it represents a rustic luxury. An object which you can truly call your own, which makes your pocket bulge pointlessly, which you can take out from time to time, not to use, but just to experience the simple pleasure of feeling it, looking at it, opening and closing it. Within the freedom of the present lurks the past. For a few seconds you become both the bucolic grandfather with his white moustache, and the child at the water's edge where the scent of elder trees lingers. In the time it takes to open and close the blade, you're not so much caught between two ages as straddling them. Therein lies the secret of the knife.

A Sunday Morning Box of Pastries

A BOX CRAMMED FULL of little individual pastries. One cream puff, one chocolate éclair, two strawberry tarts and one vanilla slice. You've chosen most of them with specific people in mind, but you're still hesitating over that extra one for the gluttons. You take your time with each request. Armed with a pair of pastry tongs, the assistant dives submissively towards the objects of your desire. She remains unflustered, even when forced to change boxes because the vanilla slice won't fit. The box, of course, has an integral role to play. Flat, with a square base and sides that fold into a curve, it forms the foundations of a fragile edifice contemplating a troubled future.

"I think that's everything."

On cue, the assistant smothers the box in a pyramid of pink paper, and then ties it up with brown ribbon. You support the parcel from underneath while paying, but as soon as you're out of the door you grab hold of it by the string, swinging it gently away from your body. That's more like it. Sunday pastries are made to be swung like a pendulum. High priest of tiny rites, you tread the fine line between arrogance and humility. This solemn show of piety, almost Magi-like, can seem a touch absurd. But your hanging pyramid is just as much a feature of the lazy Sunday pavements as the occasional leek that can be spied poking out of a shopping bag.

With a box of pastries in one hand, you cut a figure like Professor Calculus in *Tintin*—the perfect cover for braving the chattering crowds on their way back from mass, and the billowing smoke from the betting shops, cafés and bars. Sundays with the family, Sundays past, Sundays present—time hangs, as if in a censer suspended by a length of brown ribbon. A slight stain appears on the outside of the box—that'll be the cream puff.

Helping Shell Peas

It ALWAYS HAPPENS AT that low ebb of the morning when time stands still. The breakfast leftovers have been cleared, the smell of lunch simmering on the stove is still some way off and the kitchen is as calm as a church. Laid out on the waxed tablecloth: a sheet of newspaper, a pile of peas in their pods and a salad bowl.

Somehow you never manage to get in on the start of the operation. You were just passing through the kitchen on your way to the garden, to see if the mail had arrived, when . . .

"Is there anything I can do to help?"

As if you didn't already know the answer. Of course you can help. Just pull up a chair. Soon an invisible metronome will lull you into the cool hypnotic rhythm

of shelling peas. The operation itself is deliciously simple. Use your thumb to press down on the join and the
pod instantly opens itself, docile and yielding. For reluc-
tant peas who disguise their youth with shriveled skin,
use the nail of your index finger to make an incision that
will rip open the green and expose all the moisture and
firm flesh beneath. You can send those little green balls
rolling out at the push of a finger. The last one is un-
believably tiny. Sometimes you can't resist crunching it.
It tastes bitter, but fresh as an eleven o'clock kitchen
where the water runs cold and the vegetables have just
been peeled—nearby, next to the sink, naked carrots
glisten on the dish towel where they've been left to dry.

You talk in little snippets of conversation, the words
welling up from the calm inside you, and again an invisible music seems to be at play. Occasionally you raise
your head at the end of a sentence, to look at the other
person; they, of course, keep their head lowered—it's
all part of the code.

You talk about work, about plans, about feeling
tired—steering clear of anything psychological. Shelling peas isn't a time to explain things, it's a time to go
with the flow, in a detached sort of way. You're looking
at five minutes' worth of work, but the pleasure lies in
rolling up your sleeves and making the moment last,
slowing down the morning pod by pod. You plunge
your hand into the contents of the salad bowl and let

the peas trickle through your fingers. They're delicate as liquid, all those contiguous round shapes in a pea-green sea, and you're actually surprised to discover that your hands aren't wet. A long, fulfilled silence, and then: "Right, all we need now is someone to go and get the bread . . ."

A Glass of Port

It ATTRACTS HYPOCRISY from the outset: "Just a small glass of port, then . . ."

You hesitate ever so slightly, as if having to make an effort to be convivial. Far be it from you to behave like those killjoys who always turn down the offer of an apertif. But the tone of your "just a small glass, then" is concessionary rather than enthusiastic. You'll play the game with a show of restraint: *mezza voce,* indulging only in furtive sips.

Port should be sipped and not drunk. This is partly because of its velvet body, and partly by way of parsimonious affectation. Let others abandon themselves to the bitter triumphs of whiskey on the rocks or dry martini. Port drinkers appreciate the tepid warmth of the fading aristocracy, the taste of fruit from the curate's garden and the old-fashioned sickliness of a recipe that brings a delicate blush to a young lady's cheeks.

The two "o"s make gullies in the black base of the bottle. *Porto.* It's as if you can hear it rolling towards the bottom of a dark abyss, below the lofty arch of a *cavalheiro's* head. Both aristocratic and ecclesiastical, it embodies the time-honored contradiction of austerity and gold. But caught in a glass, the darkness becomes a memory. More garnet than ruby-colored, this viscous lava whispers tales of knives, of vengeful suns and convents put to the dagger. So much violence within the ritual of one small glass, within the prudence of dainty mouthfuls. A taste of burnished suns and stifled blows. A twisted taste of dark fruit, in which excess and brilliance drown. Each sip marks a partial return to the fiery source. Like a pleasure in reverse, only fully appreciated as sobriety gives way to deceit. Each time you swallow, the weight of that velvet registers more strongly. Red and black. Each mouthful embracing a lie.

The Smell of Apples

THE MOMENT YOU GO down into the cellar, it hits you. So many apples, neatly stacked on upturned crates. So many memories. Not that this sudden rush of nostalgia was part of the plan. But what can you do? The smell is overwhelming. How could you have strayed so far from the bittersweet taste of childhood?

The wizened ones are the tastiest, a rich flavor locked within the wrinkles of that cheating skin. Not that you'd dream of eating them. That would mean transforming the suggestion of a smell into the reality of a taste. For beyond the wonderful potency of that scent lurks something more profound, something from within. The whiff of a better self. Autumn term. A page of scratchy downstrokes and upstrokes in blue ink. Rain beating on the roof, and a long evening ahead of you . . .

The smell of apples is more than a taste of the past. Its pungent intensity may transport you back in time, to a saltpetered cellar, a dark attic. But its secret lies in making you live the past within the present. Behind you, overgrown grass in a damp orchard. Ahead a warm breeze hovers in the shade. The smell fuses every shade of brown and red, with just a hint of acid green. It captures the essence of the skin's softness, its subtle coarseness. Even though your mouth's parched, you hold back. Nothing could make you violate that white flesh. Wait for October, for the ploughed earth, the dankness of the cellar and the rain. The smell of apples is painful. It evokes a life of fortitude and patience, which we're no longer capable of recognizing.

A Croissant in the Street

You were the first
to wake. Subtle as a sleuth, you dressed and tiptoed
from room to room. A watchmaker couldn't have
opened and closed the front door with greater preci-
sion. And here you are: outside, in the blue of a morning laced with pink. A tasteless marriage, redeemed
only by the purging cold. Each breath produces a cloud
of hot air; this early-morning pavement makes you feel
liberated and alive. You don't care that the bakery is
some way off. Jack Kerouac, with your hands in your
pockets, you strike out ahead: each step is a celebration.
You surprise yourself by walking on the curb as if you
were a child again, as if it were the edge that counted,
the boundary of things. This is time in its purest

essence, this fragment filched from the day while everyone else is asleep.

Or almost everyone. You're relying, of course, on the warm light of the bakery over there; it's actually neon, but the idea of warmth gives it an amber glow. There has to be just the right amount of condensation on the window as you approach, just the right twinkle in the eye of the baker's wife, reserved exclusively for her first customers. Complicity at daybreak.

"Five croissants, please, and a baguette that's not too crusty."

The baker appears in his floury vest at the back of the shop and greets you as one would a comrade in the hour of combat.

Back outside on the street, you can feel it already: the walk home is never the same. The pavement is less free somehow, the journey more mundane with a baguette tucked under one elbow, a bag of croissants in your hand. But then you decide to take one of the croissants out of the bag. Still warm and gooey. You indulge in a little gluttony on the move, to combat the cold: as if the heart of the winter morning were crescentshaped and you were its oven, its haven. Heavy with yellow, you slow down as you encounter the blue, the gray, the fading pink. The best part is already over and the day is just beginning.

The Noise of a Dynamo

PERFECT FRICTION—A dynamo skimming and scraping as it purrs against the wheel. How long since you last rode a bicycle in the faltering light of dusk? A car honks its horn as it overtakes, and before you know it you're back in the old routine. Leaning backwards, left hand dangling, you press the dynamo into place, keeping your fingers clear of the spokes. A moment of sweet consent as the bottle shape meets the wheel. The slender yellow beam of the front light turns the night blue. And then the music strikes up. That constant reassuring whir. With each push of the pedal you generate power. It's a peculiar sensation, nothing like the grating of a mudguard. The rubbery adhesion of a tire against the grooves of a dynamo is less a hindrance than a deliciously drowsy invitation. All around you, the countryside succumbs.

Vivid memories of childhood mornings—cycling to school and the tingling recollection of frozen fingers. Summer evenings when you went to collect milk from the neighboring farm—the little metal can with its loose chain rattling about in rhythmic counterpoint. Starting out on fishing trips at dawn, behind you the silence of the sleeping house, the delicate clatter of fishing rods. A dynamo can carve a path of freedom through the wispish gray, the not-quite-purple of the half-light. It sets a gentle, steady pace, attuned to the action of wheel and chain. And so you advance like a wind machine, stirring up the breezes of memory lane.

An Inhalation

Do you remember when you were ill as a child, those days you used to spend in bed, reading your favorite comic books? It seems that the older you get, the less fun you have being ill. You can always resort to a hot toddy, of course. Never underestimate a stiff toddy and a good whine. An inhalation, on the other hand, offers the sensual gratification of an altogether more subtle luxury.

It always takes awhile to come round to the idea. To get beyond that bitter, faintly poisonous initial impression. Inhalations make you think of gargling and that stale leathery aftertaste. But your head's throbbing so hard, and you're feeling so groggy. Perhaps a little convalescence in the kitchen isn't such a bad idea after all.

Let the functional environment of the stove, the sink and the fridge soothe you. Your eye alights on the bottle of menthol inhalant, up there on the shelf, next to the tea bags and the herbal infusions. Its old-fashioned label depicts a beaming face inhaling a spiral of snowy white steam. That clinches it. This is your chance to revive an outdated custom.

You begin by heating the water. There used to be a special plastic inhaler, but it always fell apart, and left red marks under your eyes anyway. You could read at the same time though, if you were prepared to hold your book far enough away. But the inhaler has long since disappeared, and you don't miss it. Just pour the boiling water into a bowl, add a spoonful of magic potion, and a greenish cloud instantly diffuses. With a towel over your head, the journey into the underworld can begin. From the outside, you look like you're taking a sensible course of action. Underneath, it's a different story. Your brain turns to pulp as you sink into a sweaty confusion. Beads of sweat clamber towards your temples. But the real action's happening on the inside. Deep regular breathing, necessary to unblock the sinuses, clears the way for the corrupting influence of menthol. Beneath that motionless exterior, an amphibian negotiates the pale underworld of a poisonous green jungle. Water becomes steam becomes water. You merge into the mist, sluggish and distended. Close at hand, in a far-away reality, you can hear a meal being prepared. But immersed in the steamy underworld of internal fevers, you've lost all desire to surface.

We Could Almost Eat Outside

I~T'S~ ~THE~ *ALMOST* ~THAT~
counts, and the use of the conditional. The suggestion
seems absurd at first. It's only the beginning of March
and there's been nothing but rain, wind and showers all
week. And now this. Since this morning, the sun's been
shining with a sort of dull intensity, a calm persistence.
Lunch is ready, and the table's been laid. But everything
seems different somehow, even inside. The window's
slightly ajar, there's an audible hum from outside and
the air feels fresh.

"We could almost eat outside." The phrase always
comes at precisely the same point in time. When it's too
late to change things because everyone's just about to sit
down, and the tablecloth's already been spread and the
first course set out. Too late? The future's what you

make of it. Perhaps you'll all feel the mad urge to grab a sweater, rush outside, wipe down the garden table like people possessed, and direct the stunned offers of help towards shaping the general mayhem. Or perhaps you'll collectively resign yourselves to eating inside in the warmth—after all, the chairs are too damp and the grass is so overgrown . . .

It doesn't matter. What does matter is the moment in which you articulate that little phrase. *We could almost . . .* A perfect existence, the one lived in the conditional tense, like those childhood games of "What if . . . ?" A world of make-believe pitted against life's certainties. The freshness of something only a hand's span away, something you almost experienced. A simple fantasy, involving the relocation of a domestic ritual. A tiny breeze of delirious wisdom which changes everything and nothing . . .

Sometimes you catch yourself saying: "We could almost have . . ." The jaded phrase of adults who've opened Pandora's box to discover only nostalgia inside. But then one of those days comes along when you catch a possibility as it passes, grasp the fragile instinct behind a hesitation, without tipping the balance. One of those days when you could almost . . .

Blackberry Picking

An END-OF-SUMMER outing, in the company of old friends. The holidays are almost over, with just a few days to go before everything starts up again, so it's good to make the most of this final stroll, which already smells of September. No need to organize it ahead of time, or to eat together. Just pick up the telephone after Sunday lunch:

"Would you like to come blackberry picking?"

"How funny, we were just going to suggest the same thing."

You always go right down to the bottom of the lane, back to the same spot at the forest's edge. Each year, the brambles get thicker and more impenetrable. The leaves are a deep matte green, the stems and thorns wine-colored like the marbled paper covers of old schoolbooks.

All you need is a plastic container to protect the berries and the picking can begin. It's a random process, to be taken at a leisurely pace. You only want enough to make two or three jars of jam, for autumn breakfasts. But the real prize is blackberry sorbet, to be eaten on the evening it's made, the last sleepy rays of summer captured within its frozen lushness.

Blackberries should be small and shiny black. But you enjoy tasting the slightly acidic reddish ones along the way. In no time your hands are stained with black and wiping them on the bleached summer grass doesn't help. At the forest's edge, russet ferns shower down droplets of purple mist from crook-shaped heads. You talk about this and that. The children grow serious as they tell you how scared or excited they are at the prospect of having a particular teacher. Summer is always brought to a close by children, and that path through the blackberry bushes will always taste of school. It's gentle underfoot, and chatter comes easily. The light between two downpours is warm and intensified. When you go blackberry picking, you harvest the summer as well. Turning the bend towards the hazel trees, you slip-slide into autumn.

The First Sip of Beer

THE ONLY ONE THAT counts. Everything that follows is bland by comparison, a tepid coating of your tongue. The harder you swallow, the more meaningless the excess. Perhaps, within the tragedy of the final sip, you can begin to recapture . . .

The first gulp! Its journey is already well advanced by the time it reaches your throat. With a frothy trail of foaming gold around your lips, bitter happiness slowly permeates your palate. It seems to last a small eternity, that first sip. You drink without hesitation, gulled by your own instinct. The ritual is familiar enough: the right quantity to ensure a perfect prelude; the instant rush of well-being, punctuated by a contented sigh, a smack of the lips, or silence; the giddy sensation of pleasure teetering on the brink of infinity . . . And yet you know that the best is already over. You put your glass down on the beer mat and push both slightly away. Time to relish the color—ersatz honey, cold sun. If only you were patient and wise enough to grasp the miracle behind this disappearing act. You notice with satisfaction that the brewer's name on the side of the glass corresponds with the beer you ordered. But whatever the relation of the vessel to its contents, nothing can bridge the gap between them, or conjure liquid out of thin air. What wouldn't you give to capture and encode the secret of pure gold? Instead, you sit at your sun-splashed white table, like a frustrated alchemist intent on keeping up appearances—each mouthful is a falling away from pleasure. Happiness has a bitter taste when you have to drink in order to forget the first sip.

The Highway at Night

THE CAR IS A STRANGE machine: home and spaceship rolled into one. A packet of mints lies comfortably within reach, while on the dashboard, phosphorescent spots glow: electric green, ice blue, pale orange. No need for the radio—later on perhaps, in time for the midnight news. Surrender yourself to the space. Of course, everything seems compliant enough, obedient to your command: gearshift, steering wheel, a quick flick of the windshield wipers, a touch on the window switch. But at the same time it feels as if the car is imposing itself on you. Driving you. A lonely figure insulated by silence. It's as if you're at the cinema, experiencing not just the film flickering before you, but a sense of bodily detachment.

The calm seems to extend outside, within the compass of the headlights, between the guardrail on one side and the bushes on the other. Open the window, however, and reality deals a blow to drowsiness. What hits you in the face is sheer speed. Like a cannonball hurtling along at seventy-five miles per hour.

You're driving through the night. The staggered signs—Futuroscope, Poitiers-Nord, Poitiers-Sud, next exit Marais Poitevin—have those quintessentially French names that remind you of geography lessons. Not that they'll ever amount to anything more than a blurred impression, a fleeting reality, hastily forgotten as you revert to old tricks. Foot on the accelerator and one eye on the speedometer, you annihilate this virtual France, and it becomes just one more lesson you'll never learn.

Service station in six miles. You decide to stop. A low cathedral of light is already discernible in the distance, looming out of the horizon like the harbor lights at the end of a voyage. Premium unleaded. Outside, there's a fresh wind blowing. The nozzle clicks into compliance, the meter whirs. In the cafeteria, you recognize the same sticky atmosphere found in every train station and nocturnal haunt. One espresso, with sugar. It's just the idea of coffee that matters, not the taste. Warmth and bitterness. A few tottering steps, an unsteady gaze, a few silhouettes across your path, but nothing said. Then you're reunited with your vehicle, like a snail with its shell. Not drowsy now. Who cares if dawn is still a long way off?

An Old Train

I T ' S DEFINITELY NOT A
TGV. Not even a turbo-train, or an Inter-City. No.
What's just pulled up is one of those old khaki-colored
trains from the sixties. You were expecting electric doors
and the clinical layout of an open car. But they've de-
cided to drag an antique locomotive out of retirement
for the day. On this of all lines. Ours not to reason why.

You make your way along the corridor. Having to
push open the door to a compartment changes everything. A blast of stale electric heat greets you. As you
break in on the intimacy of a cozy but exclusive atmosphere, you're scrutinized from head to toe. Forget the
anonymity of open cars. Here, failing to greet your fellow passengers is considered barbaric. As is neglecting
to ask if a seat is taken. Correct etiquette also dictates a

hint of morose anxiety. Which is the secret password. A consensus of rumbling stomachs marks your acceptance into the family bosom.

You're now free to settle yourself into the seat next to the corridor and stretch out your legs. Each glance between fellow passengers adheres to a complex but instinctive gymnastics. You're allowed to focus on the black rubbery floor between people's feet, or to fix your stare just above head level. Anything in between— needless to say the most interesting area—is to be approached with extreme caution. Don't think you can fool anyone: a glinting eye betrays a modest gaze. Better go for the safe option and take in the scenery, with a stop-off at the lead ashtrays engraved with "SNCF." But it's higher up, near the studded mirror, that your gaze comes comfortably to rest. Not that the black-and-white print of Moustiers-Sainte-Marie (Hautes-Alpes) in its metal frame offers any possibility of escape. It only reinforces the impression of a bygone era, of compartmental etiquette and packed lunches. You can almost smell the *saucisson* cut with an Opinel pocketknife, almost picture the red-and-white-checked napkin. You're back in a time when travel meant adventure, when there was always someone on the platform to meet you and ask the right questions.

"No, I was fine. Yes, a corridor seat . . . A young couple, two soldiers and an old man who got out at Aubrais."

The Tour de France

THE TOUR DE FRANCE means summer. Endless summer, scorched by the meridian July heat. Inside, the Venetian blinds are down and life takes on a slower pace as shafts of sunlight catch the dancing dust. It's bad enough staying indoors when the sky is such a deep blue. But it seems crazy to flop in front of the television, when the forests look so lush and the water sparkles so tantalizingly. And yet you're watching the Tour de France. You're respecting a ritual, not indulging in wanton idleness. And you're not just watching this year's Tour de France. You're watching all the Tours de France ever. Each shot of the *peloton* heading along the roads of Auvergne or Bigorre recalls all the packs from the past. Old-fashioned woolens hide just beneath the surface of those fluorescent outfits—

Anquetil's yellow, embroidered with the "Helyett" insignia; the blue-white-red of the short-sleeved Roger Rivière; the dark purple and yellow of Raymond Poulidor, sponsored by Mercier-BP-Hutchinson. In place of those disk wheels, you see tubular tires slung across the shoulders of Lapébie or René Vietto. The teeming tarmac of L'Alpe-d'Huez gives way to the lonely scree of La Forclaz.

Someone always says: "What I really like about the Tour is the scenery."

You travel across an overheated and festive France, people strung out in a thin ribbon along her plains, towns and mountain passes. The osmosis between man and environment looks like child's play, at times overexcited and fanatical. But a bit of ribald humor to offset the stony backdrop of Galibier, or the mists of Tourmalet, only serves to heighten the mythical dimension of our heroes.

The flat stages may be less decisive, but watching them is all part of the ritual. Everything becomes more compact, with the prize for ingenious maneuvers going to the press. Surprise upsets have little impact on the overall rankings. What matters is the idea of the whole of France coming together in the time of sunshine and harvest, even if only for a moment. One summer looks very much like another on the television screen. The most exciting moments taste of mint cordial.

A Banana Split

OF COURSE YOU'D NEVER
eat one normally. Too hideous, too over-the-top and
sickly. But there it is. Recently you've had your fill of
sharp-tasting desserts in delicate colors. You've ven-
tured as far as "floating-island pudding" for sweets of the
so-light-you-hardly-notice-them variety and got no further with summer specialties than "the four red fruits in
season." So, for once, you don't skip the line on the
menu.

"What will you have?"

"A banana split."

It's never easy to order this mountain of simple pleasure. The waiter notes your request with professional
deference, but you can't help feeling sheepish. There's
something childish in the whim, something which re-

sists both dietary and aesthetic objections. Banana splits are all about basic appetite, about puerile and provocative gluttony. As the waiter brings it to you, neighboring tables cast incredulous glances at your plate. A banana split is served either on a dinner plate or in an enormous boatlike dish, neither of which is remotely discreet. At other tables diners are eating out of slender dishes made for storks, nibbling at thin slices of chocolate cake on dainty saucers. But banana splits like to spread themselves. It's all part of their earthy appeal. A halfhearted attempt to pile the banana up on top of the chocolate and vanilla scoops does little to reduce the surface area, the problem exacerbated by a generous dollop of whipped cream. There are millions of people in this world dying of hunger. You can just about entertain such a sobering thought in front of a slab of dark chocolate. But confronted with a banana split? As the apparition spreads before your eyes, you suddenly realize you're no longer hungry.

Fortunately, remorse sets in, and you soldier on with your decadent choice. A healthy sense of defiance comes to the rescue of your waning appetite. You're breaking the rules again, like the naughty child who used to steal jars of jam from the pantry, only this time you've managed to flaunt a forbidden pleasure before the world of grown-ups. Right through to the last spoonful, it's a sin.

Potluck

Honestly, it wasn't planned. You still had some work to do for the next day. In fact, you'd only popped over to ask about something, and then it happened:

"How about joining us for some supper? But you'll have to take potluck."

You relish those few seconds in which you sense the offer coming. It's not just a case of prolonging an enjoyable experience, but of pushing back the barriers of time. The day's been so predictable and the evening looks set to run according to plan. Then, suddenly, within the space of a few seconds, life takes on a new lease: the course of events can be altered, just like that. Of course, you say yes.

Evenings like this are, by their very nature, informal.

Not for you a ceremonial aperitif and the sitting-room armchair. In the kitchen, the conversation bubbles away.

"Would you mind giving me a hand with the potatoes?"

Armed with a vegetable peeler, you can talk frankly, without inhibition. You munch a radish, almost one of the family, part of the household. Relaxed. You can move about freely. You've earned the right to poke around in cupboards and hidden nooks. Where did you say you keep your mustard? The mingling smell of parsley and shallots reminds you of another time, a forgotten closeness—those evenings when your homework was spread out on the kitchen table, perhaps?

The words begin to falter. No need to force the flow. Real pleasure lies in appreciating the spaces between. No awkwardness. A library book catches your attention, and you begin to flick through it. Suddenly you hear a voice saying: "I think that's everything." You turn down an aperitif. Right decision. Before you eat, there's still time to chat around the table, your feet resting on the stretcher of a rush-seated chair. As an impromptu guest, you feel free to unwind. The black cat curled up in your lap seems to have adopted you. It's as if life itself had accepted the invitation to take potluck, and in so doing come to a complete standstill.

Reading on the Beach

N̄O ONE EVER SAID THAT
reading on the beach was easy. If you're lying on your
back, it's almost impossible. You have to hold the book
at arm's length, directly above your face, in order to
block out the sun's glare. Which is fine for a few minutes, until you feel the urge to shift. So you try lying on
your side instead, propped up on an elbow, with one
hand to screen your forehead and the other to hold the
book open and turn the pages. This proves equally un-
comfortable. You finish up on your stomach, holding
the book out in front of you. There's always a slight
breeze at ground level. Tiny mica crystals insinuate
themselves into the binding. Those grains of sand which
cluster on the flimsy gray pages of paperbacks soon lose
their sparkle and get forgotten—a little excess weight

to be flicked away every so often. But when it comes to the thick white paper you find in hardbacks, the same grains really dig their way in. Sand sinks into the creamy ridges, glinting here and there. Like extra punctuation, opening up new horizons.

The subject matter of the book should be given careful thought. A curious pleasure can be found in contrasts. Read that bit in Léautaud's *Journal* where he rails against the bodies littering the beaches of Brittany. Read Proust's *Within a Budding Grove,* and reacquaint yourself with a lost world of bathing and boaters, of parasols and polite introductions. Escape the heat by immersing yourself in the grimy rain of *Oliver Twist.* Gallop through the heavy stillness of July, like d'Artagnan in *The Three Musketeers.*

Not that there's anything wrong with matching the local color. Let your own desert expand the horizons of Le Clézio's *Le Desert* and the sprinkling of sand on the page soon hides the secrets of the Saharan Touareg, shrouded in slow blue shadows.

After a long stretch, your chin starts to disappear into the sand and you end up drinking the beach. So you reposition yourself, arms folded against your chest, one hand free to slide out and turn or fold the corner of the page as necessary. Reading becomes a melancholic experience, at once superficial and profound—almost adolescent. You can't read on the beach without adopt-

ing this series of contortions, without reconciling yourself to these various attempts and failures, these irra-
tional urges. You feel as if you're reading with your
whole body.

Real Turkish Delight

Have you ever been given Turkish delight in one of those white wooden boxes, with a pattern scorched into the lid? The tacky sort someone brought back from their holiday, or else rushed out and bought as a last-minute present. The sort that will never arouse desire. That comes with a plastic sheet coated in icing sugar, preventing the pieces sticking together and inhibiting the sensual pleasure of picking them up with your fingers. The sort of Turkish delight you eat after coffee, dubiously sinking an incisor into its flesh as your free hand brushes icing sugar from your sweater.

Let's face it, Turkish delight only tastes any good

when it's bought and enjoyed in the street. You catch sight of it in the window. A pyramid of the real stuff, modestly displayed between boxes of henna and the almond green, sugary pink and golden yellow of Tunisian sweets. The shop looks narrow, crammed full from floor to ceiling. You shuffle in with a mixture of shyness and arrogance, and a smile that's too polite to be true, unsure of yourself and your surroundings. Does the boy with the frizzy hair work here, or is he a friend of the boss's son? Not so long ago, you could enter confident of being served by a Berber in a blue beret. But now you have to approach the situation blindly, unable to disguise what you really are—a helpless, greedy philistine. You're still confused as to whether or not the boy really is an assistant, but he's prepared to sell and you're beginning to feel acutely uneasy. Six pieces? Certainly. A pink one? Or all pink. If that's what you want. Your embarrassment is heightened by a casual obsequiousness that smacks of mockery. But the "assistant" has already wrapped your pieces of pink Turkish delight in a paper bag. You cast a bewildered eye over a treasure trove packed with chickpeas and Sidi Brahim wine, where even the stack of red cocoa boxes has a cabalistic feel to it. You pay up, defeated, and like a thief you slink out, bag in hand. But outside on the pavement, a few yards further on, you reap your just reward. The Turkish delight you buy from a corner shop is made to be eaten on the quiet and in the street, in the cool of the evening—who cares if you get icing sugar on your sleeves?

Sunday Evening

SUNDAY EVENING. NO one can be bothered to set the table, or to prepare a proper supper. You take it in turns to wander into the kitchen and make a Sunday evening snack—a cold chicken sandwich with mustard should hit the spot, washed down with a glass of claret to finish off the bottle. Your friends left at six o'clock. A long selvedge of evening lies ahead. You run a bath. A real Sunday evening bath, with lots of bubbles and plenty of time to unwind, until all you're left with is a shrinking foam island on either side of you. The bathroom mirror mists over and your thoughts soften. Don't mull over the week just gone and certainly don't contemplate the week to come. Warmth and humidity have made your fingers wrinkly and the foamy drips hanging off them begin to mesmerize you. As the last of the water runs out, it's time to extricate yourself. What next? A book? Later on, perhaps. Right now, the television beckons. The more trashy the program, the better. You relish being able to watch just for the sake of watching, without having to justify your behavior. Like the bathwater, this weekly ritual numbs you as it pampers. In your mind's eye, you're already in slippers, you feel so comfortably set up for the rest of the evening. And that is precisely the point when a twinge of sadness makes its entrance. Gradually, the television becomes intolerable and you switch it off. Your thoughts drift, sometimes right back to childhood—hazy memories of counting each step on walks spent worrying about school and longing for romance. You feel overwhelmed. The upheaval in your soul is as strong as summer rain, washing across you in familiar waves of joy and sorrow—this is what Sunday evening is all about. Every Sunday evening you've ever experienced fixed inside this bubble. Like photographs developed in bathwater.

The Travelator at
Montparnasse Station

TIME LOST, OR TIME gained? Whichever way you look at it, this silent rolling walkway imposes a long hiatus in the course of its unswerving journey. As if it were an apology for the cruel existence of such an epic stretch. Even slaves to urban stress deserve some respite. But only on the condition that they stick together, making this blurred passage in their odyssey an act of objective acceleration.

The travelator at Montparnasse station seems endless. People tend to approach it gingerly, as if about to step onto a shop escalator. Except that here no steps spring open like an alligator's jaw. Everything happens horizontally. A sudden rush of vertigo hits you, as if you were going down a flight of stairs in the dark and made the mistake of thinking there was still one more step left. Once embarked on this rippling stream, everything seems to jolt. Is the tension in your body generated by the walkway? Or are you reasserting yourself in order to compensate for giving in? Out in front, those in a real hurry get into top gear by taking extra-long strides. But it's far more pleasurable to remain an observer, one hand resting lightly on the moving black banister.

Sacerdotal figures glide toward you from the opposite direction. Both parties adopt the same contrived gaze. It's a strange encounter, both intimate and inaccessible; the speed with which people are carried away provokes a certain indifference. So many individual destinies captured for a second, so many blank faces fading into a gray background. To the side, the area reserved for those die-hard walkers who spurn the benefits of mechanical assistance. They charge along at breakneck speed, anxious to demonstrate the scope of other people's indolence. Ignore them: their urge to make everyone else feel guilty is both primitive and absurd. Allow yourself instead to be seduced by the travelator's intrinsic charms, by this injection of feverish wisdom into a melancholy path. Caught in static flight, you become a character in a Magritte painting: an image of urban banality on an endless conveyor belt, gliding past fleeting mirror images of yourself.

A Trip to the Cinema

YOU DON'T REALLY GO out when you go to the cinema. In fact, you hardly make contact with anyone at all. Going into the auditorium, you're insulated, walking on air. The film hasn't started yet. Aquarium lighting keeps muted conversations in check. Everything is curved, velvet, muffled. Your feet glide effortlessly over the carpet as you head towards a row of empty seats. It wouldn't be accurate to describe your next action as sitting down, nor yet as settling into your seat. The challenge is to tame that over-stuffed volume, and then curl up sensuously, in stages. Communal activity and private pleasure converge as you turn to face the screen.

And that's about as far as you get in terms of social interaction. What clues will you ever get to the character of that oblivious giant three rows ahead, still buried in his newspaper? A few laughs, perhaps, at jokes you've missed. Or, even worse, silence when you're in stitches. You don't go to the cinema to find yourself. You go to hide, to snuggle up, to vanish. You're at the bottom of a pool and who knows what might come swimming out of the blue, from that mock stage? Odorless and draft-free, the auditorium tilts towards a hazy one-dimensional expectancy. So much volume devoted to a single surface.

Darkness falls around you as the altar lights up. You begin to float like a fish on the wing, or a bird in water. Your body grows numb as you merge into the English countryside, the streets of New York, the rain in Brest. You are life and death, war and love, caught in a funnel of dancing dust, where a giant brush paints sweeping strokes of light.

As the final credits roll your body remains prostrate, breath caught. Then comes the shock of the lights. Time to wrench yourself away from the padded comfort, to dust yourself off and sleepwalk toward the exit. Don't say anything on your way out, certainly don't venture an opinion. Just wait patiently on the sloping carpet for the giant with the newspaper to overtake you. Drifting like an astronaut, savor the last precious seconds in space.

An Autumn Sweater

It's always later than you think. September sped by in a back-to-school flurry. When the rain set in you finally acknowledged the arrival of autumn. Accepted that the days ahead amounted to little more than a prelude to the onset of winter. And yet, almost without knowing it, you were waiting for something. October. The first real overnight frosts, the first yellow leaves against clear blue skies. October, a warm wine, bathed in tender light, when the sun is at its best at four o'clock in the afternoon and the outline of everything is as soft as that of the pears which fall from the trellis.

Time for a new sweater. Time to dress in autumn tones: sweet chestnut, brushwood, conker husk, russula pink. Time to wear the season on your woolen sleeve. To celebrate the blaze before it burns itself out.

What about one of the greener hues? An Irish split-pea green, misty, rough as whiskey—desolate and wild, like fields of peat and cut grass. Or one of the reds? But there are so many to choose from. Pre-Raphaelite auburn and gingerbread from childhood memories; russet soil, burnt sun sky and all the shades of the forest. Colors to capture the elusive smell of fairs and trees, of wild mushrooms and water. What about a cable-knit oatmeal sweater with stitches big enough to pass for homemade?

Find a baggy sweater to swathe your body in the season. A tank top, short on sleeves and long on hope . . . It lifts the soul to play the end out in a game of colors. So go and choose an antidote to those seasonal blues. When you buy a new autumn sweater you buy the color of the day.

On Hearing a Piece of News
in the Car

"FRANCE INTER, IT'S FIVE o'clock and time for the news read by . . ." A snatch of music, then: "Good evening. The news has just come in that Jacques Brel is dead."

At this point the highway begins a steep descent into a nondescript valley, somewhere between the exits for Évreux and Mantes. You must have taken this route a hundred times before, with nothing on your mind but how to overtake a heavy-goods vehicle, whether you've got the right change for the tollbooth. Suddenly the landscape jumps out at you, captured in a single image. Like a photograph it all happens in a split second. This gray, anonymous three-lane slope heading toward the Seine Valley assumes a character, a particularity, that you'd never have dreamed possible. Perhaps even the red and blue Antar truck in the slow lane will be caught in the frame. It's as if you're discovering for the first time a place you previously had no desire to get to know, somewhere you always associated with a certain tedium, a faint weariness—the boring part of the journey.

The name Jacques Brel conjures up so many images, his songs bring back so many adolescent memories, you can almost feel the tidal wave of that standing ovation when he sang "Ne me quitte pas" at the Olympia Theater in 1964. All this will fade. Time moves on. There'll be plenty of airplay, not to mention various tributes in the immediate aftermath. But after the fuss has died down and the songs have trickled out, that stretch of highway through the valley will always come back to haunt you. It's absurd or magical, depending on how you look at it, and there's nothing you can do about it. Life directs its own film, as the shield becomes a cinema and the radio a camera. The flickering rushes are inside your head. The journey's left its mark, the false familiarity of those indistinguishable landscapes suddenly resolving itself. The death of Jacques Brel is a three-lane highway, with a large Antar truck in the slow lane.

A Garden in August

Summertime, early afternoon in the middle of August, and you're walking through a garden somewhere in Aquitaine. Not a breeze for miles around. Even the light seems to have fallen asleep over there by the tomatoes: a single spot illuminates the redness of each fruit. They're stained with little specks of soil from the last time it rained. You feel a sudden urge to rinse them in cold water and eat them while their flesh is still warm. Time seems to stand still as you register the subtle color variations. Some of the tomatoes are pale green, hinting at a deeper hue in their hearts, and others are almost acidic orange. Little danger of those bending the branch. Only the ripe tomatoes assume a drooping sensuality.

A ladder has been propped up against a sapling plum

tree. The path around the vegetable garden is strewn with fallen fruit. From a distance the plums look purplish, but closer inspection confirms a battle between deep blue and pink, as well as a few grains of sugar, which cling to their fragile skins. The fallen fruit bursts open, weeping apricot flesh into brown earth. Back up in the tree, patches of red have started to appear on those ochre-green plums not yet fully ripened: the blue of their older siblings both tempts and terrifies them.

You try to seek out the shade. But the sun beats resolutely down between the branches. It bleaches the vegetable garden, makes the lettuces lazy, and leaves a trail of bugs and insects spread-eagled on the ground. The only sign of resistance comes from the vigorously green carrot leaves, as if spared a languid fate by dint of their thinness. Up by the hedge at the far end, it's already too late for the raspberry bushes: ruby velvet has given way to parchment brown. Along the stone wall at the other end, a pear tree runs its branches through the trellis, the geometric pattern feminized by the shape of matte fruit freckled with red sand. But the most acidic, thirst-quenching freshness is to be found a stone's throw away, rising up from the foot of the muscat vine. The grapes themselves seem to hesitate between pale gold and sea green, between opacity and translucence; the brazen gorge on light, the timid hide behind a thin coating of dust and condensation. This flirtation between adolescent grapes and August sun is already threatened by a few wine-colored spots.

Blistering heat, but the plum tree, the apricot tree, and the cherry tree provide plenty of shade for the unused ping-pong table—a few red plums have landed on its flaking emerald paint. Blistering heat, but in the heart of August the promise of water lies curled up and asleep within the garden. The discolored hose has been wrapped around a long bamboo pole. There's something reassuringly familiar about the irregularity of its twists and curves, about the rough and ready manner in which its connections have been bound up with insulating tape and string. Its water is surely safe from the violence of lime deposits and pump. At dusk, just the right quantity of watery tenderness and wisdom will flow through it.

But for now, the sun is high in the sky and the colors—bleached yellow, green, pink—are framed with stillness. It's a time to stand and take stock.

Getting Your Espadrilles Wet

THE PATH HARDLY seems damp at all. You don't notice anything at the time, just the gentle impact of rope on earth causing the ground to tremble beneath your feet. Which is what makes walking in espadrilles such a treat. When you're in espadrilles, you're just civilized enough to be on intimate terms with the world, without the tentativeness of bare feet or well-heeled arrogance. Espadrilles mean summer, when the world is supple and warm, and tarmac starts to melt. Best of all is a sandy beaten track, just after it's rained. You can smell . . . maize fields, elder saplings and fallen poplar leaves—lazy yellow leaves snoozing in summertime at the feet of trees. A golden smell. Further on, the scent of dark green rises up from the water's edge, with a hint of mint pervading

the dull silt. Behind the poplar trees and over towards
the horizon the sky is streaked with gray and purple.
Sated, the clouds are in retreat. You appreciate the balance between the landscape, the smells and the spring
in your stride. But gradually the harmony is under-
mined: with each new stride, the ground and your feet
seem to drag the walk downwards. When it dawns on
you that your espadrilles are damp, it's already much
too late. The onslaught is relentless. A dubious ring
moving in from the edge of the material exposes the
coarseness of the fabric. And you'd fancied yourself
walking on air, swathed in linen fine enough to cut
through skin. Two puddles later, this ethereal tissue is
rough as a potato sack. It's not the humidity that rankles
so much as the heaviness. The hypocritical sole, which is
the cause of the problem, abandons the fight after a feeble show of resistance: its knotted rope wallowing in a
cruel quagmire, where nothing is allowed to breathe. Its
rubber coating may be a token concession to modern
comfort, but what's the use of flimsy protection in the
face of irremediable disaster? Espadrilles are only espadrilles, after all. Once sodden, they grow increasingly
heavy, as the smell of silt overpowers that of the
poplars. Ironically the sky no longer poses any threat
and yet you're wet, the summer cloys, the sand sticks.
And the worst is still to come. Espadrilles never really
dry out. If you leave them on a window ledge or in a

shoe cupboard, they curl up, the knotted rope expand-
ing into a sort of fluffy wadding, the cloth permanently
coarsened, the watermark forever sealed.

Those early warning signs indicate an alarming prog-
nosis: no remission, no hope. Getting your espadrilles
wet captures something of the excruciating thrill of a
complete shipwreck.

The Snowstorm Inside
a Paperweight

INSIDE EVERY PAPER-
weight, winter reigns. Pick one up. The snow floats in
slow-motion, agitated by the upward spiral of a storm.
But the blizzard, once blurred and opaque, soon abates
and the turquoise-blue sky reverts to its static melancholy. A few stray flakes linger before fluttering back
down, sucked to the bottom by a muffled laziness. As
you put the paperweight back on the shelf, you can't
help sensing that something has changed. It's as if a
voice was crying out from that vision of stillness. Every
paperweight is the same. Whether the setting is a
seascape decorated with algae and fish, the Eiffel Tower,
Manhattan, a tropical rain forest, a mountaintop, or a

souvenir from Mont Saint-Michel, the flakes still disperse and fade when the snow-dance is over. Before this winter ball, there was nothing. Afterwards, a lone flake on the Empire State Building is left, a tiny souvenir, safe from the water of passing days. The ground is strewn with delicate fragments of memory

Paperweights never forget. Silent tempests stalk their dreams. Blizzards beg to be reenacted. And yet it's their fate to be stranded on the shelf. You'll forget about the simple pleasure of falling snow in your hand, about the special power you have to rouse a world under glass from the deepest of sleeps.

Inside, the air is made of water. This doesn't strike you as odd, at first. But closer inspection reveals a tiny air bubble trapped at the top. Your perspective suddenly shifts. You're no longer looking at the Eiffel Tower, stark against an April blue sky, or at a frigate cutting through a millpond sea. Everything becomes thickly apparent: water flows at sky level, inside the glass. These desolate kingdoms of meandering sobriety and silent deluge. A milky blue paint spreads upwards from the base towards the ceiling, sky, surface. An artificially tender shade of blue, which is capable of exerting an unsettling calm despite the fact that it doesn't really exist—like those twists of fate that niggle in the quiet lull of a siesta. The world heats up quickly when you hold it in your hands. An avalanche of flakes instantly dispels the water's hidden torment. It's snowing deep inside you now, in a far-away winter where a light layer covers the substance beneath. Snow is so gentle, when it's underwater.

A Newspaper for Breakfast

A CURIOUS LUXURY. Communing with the world from the comfort of the breakfast table as you savor the aroma of fresh coffee. Wars, atrocities and natural disasters on the front page. The same news on the radio would stress you out instantly, all those chiseled sentences delivered like punches. Not so with newspapers. You spread yours out on the kitchen table as far as the toaster and the butter dish will allow. Somehow, the violence of our times doesn't have the same impact when it tastes of chocolate spread, gooseberry jam and toast. Newspapers have a sedating effect. *Libération, Le Figaro, Ouest-France, La Dépêche du Midi* . . . they tell you more about themselves than they do about the global picture. The latest disasters put in perspective by those perennial mastheads, as if giving a certain edge to the otherwise placid ritual of breakfast. The surplus of information and coffee dictates a leisurely reading pace. As you turn over slowly to reveal what the next page holds in store, it's a case of context winning out over content.

In films, newspapers are often evoked by the high-pitched frenzy of rotary presses, the hoarse cry of a street vendor. But the newspaper you collect from your mailbox first thing in the morning is an altogether more relaxed experience. For a start, it's full of yesterday's news: the present tense tempered by a good night's sleep. Information wins out over sensation. There's a certain pleasure to be derived from the abstract language of the weather forecast: instead of glancing outside for signs of how the day will turn out, you assimilate the information from inside where the weather tastes of bittersweet coffee. The sports pages, in particular, hold no surprises. The hope of revenge following hot on the heels of defeat, the sporting calendar coming round again before the losses can be accounted too great.

Nothing really happens in your morning newspaper and that's why you look forward to it so much. It's a means of prolonging your hot coffee and toast. It informs you that the world hasn't changed overnight and that the day's in no hurry to get started.

The World of Agatha Christie

ARE AGATHA CHRISTIE'S novels really so atmospheric? Perhaps, simply by saying "I'm reading an Agatha Christie," we engage in a process of invention. Rain on the lawn beyond the bow windows, mallard-green foliage on the double chintz curtains and armchairs with the sort of undulating curves you disappear into. All plausible enough, but where's the textual evidence? Where are those tea services sporting scarlet-red hunting scenes, those brittle blue Wedgewood ashtrays?

Hercule Poirot has only to tweak the waxed tips of his moustache and activate his little gray cells and hey presto: you're starting to see the translucent orange of the tea, starting to smell the insipid mauve perfume worn by old Mrs. Atkins.

There's been a murder, and yet everything remains so calm. Umbrellas have been propped up to dry in the entrance hall, a servant with milky white skin crosses the pale stretch of beeswaxed parquet. Nobody plays on the old upright anymore, but the shrill notes of a lovers' song still seem to tinkle out over the photo albums and the display of Japanese porcelain. Of course, it's the plot and tracking down the murderer that interests us most. Not the violence of the death. But there's no point in competing with Poirot's brilliance, or Agatha's artistry. She will always have the final word, will always surprise us. That's her prerogative.

Which is why you fabricate a cozy universe for yourself in that inevitable gap between the crime being committed and the culprit being exposed. English cottages are surprisingly accommodating: you can fill them with the leathery commotion of Victoria Station, with parasols redolent of tedious strolls along the pier at Brighton, even the lugubrious corridors of *David Copperfield*.

The games of croquet may be forever tinged with damp, but the evening is clear. A window has been left ajar so that the fading scent of autumn roses can waft languidly over the bridge players. The hunting season will soon be upon us, with its backdrop of russet-colored brambles and elder hedges.

The novelist, of course, remains silent about all that.

So, we behave as is only natural in the face of oppressive authority. Sneakily, almost fraudulently, we tuck into a world of forbidden fruit. Having cooked up our own meal, we discover how delicious it is.

The Mobile Library

Everyone likes the mobile library. Once a month, it appears in the Place de la Poste. You know its schedule a year in advance, because tucked inside one of your books is a little brown card with the dates printed on it. You know that from four to six o'clock on December 17th, a big white van sporting the Council logo will keep its appointment. There's something reassuring about it. You feel safe knowing that in exactly one month's time this reading room on wheels will return to light up its spot in the square. It's even better in winter, of course, when the village lanes are deserted. Then, the mobile library becomes a real hub of excitement. Not exactly a crowd—this isn't the market, after all. But a group of familiar figures gathers around the awkward set of steps at the entrance to the van. You know that in another six months you'll encounter Michèle and Jacques ("So, have you set a date for your retirement yet?"), Armelle and Océane ("Your daughter's certainly got the eyes to live up to her name!") and others to be greeted with a knowing smile, even though you don't really know them. This ritual may be all that you have in common, but it's a bond in itself.

The van door is a strange affair. You have to squeeze between two clear plastic panels, which serve as draft excluders. Once you've made it through the airlock, you find yourself in the snug world of carpeted silence where a leisurely studiousness prevails. Both the young girl and the older librarian to whom you return your books indicate, by their greeting, that they remember you. But that is the extent of their friendliness. Everything is muffled. Nothing is allowed to disturb the silent freedom of each individual as they browse. Even if this means resorting to astonishing feats of physical dexterity in order to avoid making indecent advances. There's a wide selection to choose from. You're allowed a total of twelve items, the aim being to exercise as eclectic a choice as possible. What about a collection of prose-poems by Jean-Michel Maulpoix? *"Day darkens beneath the growing pile of falling leaves and flowers from the lime-tree."* That's enough to whet your appetite. Christopher Finch's enormous book of *Nineteenth-Century Water-*

colours will weigh you down, but a quick glance at those beautiful pre-Raphaelite redheads and Turner dawns makes you realize how fortunate you are to be able to claim seven pounds of matte luxury without having to pay for the privilege. A photography magazine with pictures by Boubat, a cassette of Bach cantatas, an album on the Tour de France. These disparate wonders find their way into your basket. It's already overladen and you'll fill it with as much again, depending on what catches your eye. Crouched down in front of the cartoons and picture books, the children can scarcely believe their luck: "The lady said I could take an extra one!"

The pace slackens off with the final choices. A smell of warm wool mixed with damp gabardine starts to rise up within the narrow space. But it's the rolling motion of the floor that you notice most of all: a subtle pitching and tossing. You'd forgotten about the tires, the movable foundations of this little shrine. The combination of warmth, seasickness and books captures the essence of winter in the country. Please note, your next appointment with the mobile library will be: Thursday, January 15th, between ten o'clock and twelve noon at the Place de L'Église, or from four until six o'clock at the Place de la Poste.

Frills Below the Counter

THE WINDOWS ARE
adorned with flowery blouses, half-cup bras, little
panties in luscious shades of sweet-pea mauve and blue,
and photos of languid models in sexy black outfits. The
cover girls look at you as if butter wouldn't melt in
their mouths, but can their candid smiles really deflect
from that wickedly silky underwear? As dens of iniquity
go, this is an unlikely contender. The most innocent of
pretexts affords you entry: "Would you mind dropping
in on Madame Rosières   I need some more buttons?"

Madame Rosières. For the proprietor of such an am-
biguous and titillating establishment, she has a prudishly
old-world name. As for all that sinful array, it's hard to
believe it could be sold by a Madame Rosières somewhere in the shadow of the corner brackets.

It was heavy and oppressive outside, a stormy, suffo-
cating heat that followed you to the newsstand and even
found its way into the pharmacy next door. But everything feels fresh as cream in Madame Rosières's shop—
the color of all those tiny sliding boxes stacked right up
to the ceiling. The shop is one long corridor, with a
counter at the far end. In the recess at the back sit two
little old women. One wears the satin dress of a
farmer's wife, and holds a straw hat with a ribbon tied
round it in her lap. The other wears blue overalls which
make her look like a schoolgirl from a bygone era. The
one in the satin dress has just popped by for a chat.
Madame Rosières is the schoolgirl. She gets up and
makes her way towards you almost too efficiently—but
you soon realize she probably welcomes this lull in her
companion's banter. Brief as it is. For your presence
does little to abate the running commentary emanating
from the satin dress, whose owner seems content to
carry on a one-way conversation.

"Well, my dear, I'm getting too old for tapestry . . ."
"You mustn't forget to give me some more embroi-
dery thread . . ."
"The poultry market's next Tuesday, isn't it . . . ?"
"This heat is just unbearable . . . !"
Towards the back of the shop, underwear gives way
to tapestry canvases: fleeing hinds, a sultry gypsy
woman, a crooner, a Brittany landscape. But the real

booty is to be found by the counter. First the buttons, every type of button imaginable, arranged in ascending order of size on little white cards. Everyday enamel ones, practical plain-cut ones; these jewels of simple refinement are best understood within the context of their natural habitat. It would be a crime to separate the pale green ones from their plum-green, emerald-green and coral-pink neighbors, just because you'd fixed on buying them. The wall display of cotton spools also has an iridescent palette of subtle color variations. Embroidery threads evince the art of nuance in secret. Secured at either end with a black paper loop and curled up in little drawers according to shade, they look like a fistful of dark snakes in Madame Rosières's hand.

And then an incongruous thought crosses your mind. Madame Rosières may have been a prize darner at school, she may be the patron saint of embroidery and the dying art of courtship, Madame Rosières may even be a stalwart defender of the sort of quality clothes you can make last forever if you keep on replacing the buttons, but is she vain enough to wear sweet-pea undergarments? You'd have thought she was the type to squeeze herself into one of those fleshy pink girdles from the market stall near her shop, the type to comfort herself with those flannel drawers stacked up next to the traditional peasant dresses.

And yet. Madame Rosières can't have spent an entire

lifetime upholding the tradition of fine lingerie without bringing some of her knowledge to bear on her own endeavors, without taking the occasional flirtatious risk. Although at her age . . . Herein, perhaps, lies the secret of an atmosphere that is at once contrived and fresh, floating in the shadow of iron brackets. If Madame Rosières were to wear a flowery blouse, it would be with the intention of satisfying neither male brutality nor the self-contemplating narcissism of a young woman. No, it would be a perfect blouse, an aesthetic blouse chosen for its flawless color and texture. Which is why this creamy temple is as fresh as if it were newly baptized. And why, despite her modest blue overalls, Madame Rosières has an imperceptible aura about her: she's the virgin queen of frills.

Looking Through
a Kaleidoscope

Dive into the reflec-
tive surfaces of this Japanese boudoir and discover a
world of secret cloisters, of light trapped within a
cylindrical cardboard prison. A theater of mysterious
shadow-play, where the wings are in the spotlight and
the walls are made of smoked glass. From the fractured
cruelty of multiple images, a miracle is born. The ends
of the cylinder don't amount to much: at one end a little peephole testifies to the banality of the voyeur; at
the other, between those two opaque circles, a hazy distance and an impression of dust conspire to make the
brightly colored crystals seem more precious. The view
from below is one-dimensional, and the gaze from
above detached. But something happens in between; in

the dark, in the unexplored terrain of a tube and beneath the cheap covering of patterned metallic paper.

Take a look. The jewels inside, brilliant blue, royal
purple, rich orange, splinter into an aqueous sea. Catch
a glimpse of an oriental glass palace, of a harem of ice
floes, of a snow crystal fit for a sultan. Embark on a
journey which changes each time you set out. Set sail
for the northern shores, on a turquoise voyage in search
of precious stones; bask in the pomegranate red of an
offshore adventure, spiced with the scent of hot gulfs.
Whole new countries suddenly appear, nameless lands
emerging from uncharted waters. You hardly have to
turn the cylinder to find yourself somewhere else, even
further away; the painful sound of rupture signifies the
heat and cold of the last country being dismantled behind you.

Not that this act of abandonment matters. A handful
of colored crystals can create a new country quickly
enough. But the final composition is never quite as
you'd envisaged. And it's that elusive difference which
makes the journey's vertigo and despair worthwhile.
You're never totally in control when it comes to this
landscape of moving crystals. The mosaic in the sky is
an original: green as an angel and red as the plush velvet
in theaters. It combines the geometric solemnity of the
Louvre gardens with the oppressive intimacy of a Chi-
nese dwelling. Whether you point the kaleidoscope in

the direction of the ceiling, wall or floor, what you see is an image of the ground, floating in the vacuum of an exploded space. Try to hold the same position as you disappear slowly into the abyss—put the tube down and the tiniest movement will destroy a continent; a single breath becomes a cyclone and the palace flies away.

Mystery unfolds in the darkest of chambers. Here, everything is weightless and fragile, lost and confused. You can never possess what you see. But if you stay still enough, you'll witness a circular revelation, catch a passing glimpse of beauty. A little fragment of wisdom and happiness between your thumb and fingers. You hardly need to touch it at all.

Calling from a Public
Phone Booth

IT STARTS WITH A SERIES
of awkward physical constraints. The heavy hypocrisy
of a door you don't know whether to push or pull, the
scrabbling around for a phone card concealed between
your Métro tickets and your driver's license—have you
got enough units left? Next, eyes glued to the display
panel, you follow instructions: *please lift the receiver . . .
please wait . . .* You feel tense and claustrophobic, and
the glass is already beginning to steam up. Dialing the
number on those metal keys provokes a series of shrill
cold tones. You feel like a prisoner in a cell. At the same
time, you know that this is all part of the initiation ritual: that through submitting to the machine you attain

the most bewildering intimacy—the human voice. Prior
to the miracle, the sound effects change. An umbilical
lament to bring you in from the cold, after those glacial
touch-tones. You make it at last to the deep pitch of a
ringing tone, pulsating like a heartbeat. Then comes the
moment of release as it cuts out.

It's only now that you lift your head. Those first
words are exquisitely ordinary and offhand. "It's me . . .
everything was fine . . . I'm just by that café in Place
Saint-Sulpice, you know the one I mean . . ."

It doesn't matter what you say, as long as you can
hear. It's extraordinary how the voice of someone you
love can betray so much—their sadness and exhaustion,
their fragility, their vitality and joy. When you have no
physical gestures to hide behind, meaning suddenly becomes transparent. A transparency which extends beyond the tedious gray of the phone booth. Only now do
you become aware of the pavement in front of you, of
the newspaper stand and the kids roller-skating, and
this sudden recognition of life beyond the glass is both
tender and magical. As if the landscape were being born
out of a distant voice. A smile finds its way to your lips.
The phone booth becomes light—it's only glass, after
all. That voice, so intimate and yet so distant, tells you
that Paris is no longer a state of exile, that pigeons are
taking off from benches, that steel can't prevail.

Cycle or Bicycle?

A CYCLE IS THE OPPO-
site of a bicycle. A fluorescent purple figure hurtling
along at forty miles an hour: cycle. Two high-school
kids cruising side by side across a bridge in Bruges: bicycle. But the distinction isn't always so clear. Michel
Audiard in knickers and long socks, stopping off to
drink a glass of dry white wine at the bar counter:
cycle. A teenager in jeans propping up their vehicle before going, book in hand, to sip mint cordial on the ter-
race: bicycle. You either belong to one camp or the
other. You can't sit on the fence. No matter how much
you try to bend the handlebar on a heavy-duty roadster,
it'll always be a bicycle. And no matter what sort of

mudguard you rig to a racer, it'll always be a cycle. You're better off declaring your allegiance than trying to disguise it. Either you carry somewhere within you the image of an idealized black sit-up-and-beg bicycle, with a scarf flapping behind you in the wind. Or you aspire to a cycle so streamlined its chain makes no more noise than a bee in flight. Bicyclists are pedestrians with added privileges, free to wander down alleyways, or to pull up at park benches when they want to read a newspaper. Cyclists never stop: surgically sealed from neck to knees in futuristic lycra, they can only waddle, so they prefer not to walk at all.

Is it a question of pace? Maybe. Although some bicyclists zoom by at high speed and some cycles are ridden by grandads who pootle along with all the time in the world. A question of weight, then? That's more like it. Intimations of flight on the one hand and a reassuring contact with the ground on the other. What else . . . ? The two camps are diametrically opposed in every way. Take the color of their clothes, for example. Cyclists wear metallic orange or Granny-Smith green, whereas bicyclists wear dull brown, off-white, matte red. Even the fabrics and shapes differ. On the one hand, loose natural fibers such as wool or velvet, perhaps even a kilt. On the other, tightly fitting synthetics.

You're born a bicyclist or a cyclist. The distinction is almost political. But cyclists have to renounce this aspect of their identity when they fall in love—you can only be in love on a bicycle.

Pétanque *for Beginners*

"So, what sort of player are you? *Tu tires, ou tu pouinntes?*"*

This feeble imitation of a Marseilles accent is all part of the game. Standing there with the balls in your hand, you experience that sinking feeling. You try to boost your morale with some lighthearted parody: you'll play the angry Raimu or the cheeky Fernandel†, and your prize will be a pastis or Fanny. But to no avail, for your lack of expertise can only ever result in a second-rate game. You don't have the flair of the first shooter who crouches down, knees slightly apart, mapping out the ideal trajectory as he cradles the ball in his hand. You'll

---

*"Are you a 'smasher' or a 'shooter'?" i.e., do you knock the other balls out of the way, or do you aim directly for the jack?
†The actors who play the two suitors in the film of Marcel Pagnol's *Fanny*.

never command the quality of silence afforded the great smasher prior to his display of brilliance—it's as if he deliberately prolongs the pause in order to highlight the triumph to come. In any case, *pétanque* is for professionals. What you're playing is the amateur version, *boules*. How many feeble aims landing a good yard short of the jack does it take, how many kamikaze shots knocking out balls you didn't want to draw, before you nudge up to the jack or score an immediate knockout?

Never mind. There's a festive buzz in the air: the summer sound of balls knocking cleanly together. You begin to pick up the language.

"What d'you reckon?"

You head over, using the tip of your shoe to indicate where the jack is hidden between two white pebbles. There's less banter now, and you become more focused. Instead of holding back and waiting your turn at the edge of the circle, you position yourself where the action is, close to the balls already in play.

"Has it taken the lead?"

You bring the piece of string over. Everyone else gathers round. With so many critical eyes fixed on you, it's a feat in itself not to hit anything while you're measuring.

"It's ahead all right. There's not much in it, though!"

You try to adopt a casual saunter on your way back to the last ball. You're not enough of a stickler to get down on your knees, but you take your time, playing the ball with slow ceremony. You watch it take its course for a second. Then, as it reaches the end of its journey, you head over, remembering to appear modestly dismissive of your achievements. It won't take the lead, but it's in the running and at least you haven't disgraced yourself.

At the beginning of the game, it was you who tended to pick up other people's balls. But now that you've made your mark, you only collect your own.